THE ZIMBABWEAN

DREAM

A journey of wealth creation rather than poverty reduction.

KELVIN TANYARADZWA SAUNGWEME

Disclaimers

- This book does not replace the advice of a medical professional. Consult your physician before making any changes to your diet or regular health plan.

- These are my perspective, and I have tried to represent events as faithfully as possible.

- The information in this book was correct at the time of publication, but the Author does not assume any liability for loss or damage caused by errors or omissions.

Address:
60 Chimoio Road
Manicaland, Rusape, Zimbabwe
Email Address:kevysaungweme@gmail.com

Contact Details:
Mobile number:(+263) 77 672 5465
Landline:(+263) 252052024

First Edition

V 2.0.1

The book is dedicated to my loving family and

friends around the world.

Contents

Foreword

My dream for Zimbabwe is for it to become a wealth powerhouse in the whole of Africa in the coming decades. I have come to believe the platitude that this statement has carried since the country's independence in 1980. With all the great leaders that we had, I am not an ingrate to fail and acknowledge their great contribution to the economy of Zimbabwe but a deficit of vision has led us as a nation to where we stand. I was livid as l made a primary assessment of the country's potential and resources that we have. Tangible and non-tangible resources to be specific, l am not going to dive deep into the politics of the country because of the vitriol nature that arose after independence for the acquisition of land by the two races that ate from the belly of the motherland Zimbabwe. My goal and main mission behind this book are to mobilize the country in a bull's eye target for a journey of wealth creation rather than poverty reduction because that has been our vivid target since independence. This book contains non-ubiquitous information but rather observations and plans for the future of citizens of Zimbabwe 10-20 years from now and how we can be prepared as a nation to see our vision of wealth creation come to pass. The author has identified our primary needs and threats to come our way if we fail to act now. Each section will contain criteria of a need or a threat and the solutions we can implement to rectify the need and threat. The readers of all walks of life that see these prerequisites as identified and elucidated below as solutions to their current problems can freely implement the ideas into their societies. The book is non-disingenuous hence it can shed a little light on our country and cultivate our economist, industrialist to subjugate our current problems and future needs by thinking innovatively, creatively with the ability to adapt to any change in phase of the global industry. I hope this foreword wasn't inane on my laconic subject matter.

KELVIN TANYARADZWA

SAUNGWEME

Rusape, Manicaland

February 2020

CHAPTER 1: THE DREAM

On a Friday afternoon whilst reciting to myself the General Laws of Physics, I questioned myself as my eyes seemed distant to my thoughts. I asked myself what l hoped Zimbabwe would be and what would make me very happy in the 20th Century. I listed my list as follows:

1. To sell a billion in stock of jewelry to America

2. To export cars and rice to Asia

3. To export medicine to India

4. To industrialize and create excess employment gaps so that foreign citizens can apply for jobs in my country

5. To also export bread and mealie meal to my African countries

6. To be the energy source of Africa

The question that preceded my co-pending list was why we were not doing that already. I brainstormed and generated a hypothesis to the real reality behind stagnant economic growth. Since we are amongst the top 2 countries in the world with the highest literacy rate, why wasn't our education solving our problems? I found no use of any citizen or generally students to go to school if they finish the 4 years or 7years courses and still fail to contribute exponentially to the GDP of the country. So should we blame the students or the school system? Can you stand and call it to suicide when the system is pulling the trigger, giving the courses but failing to provide the jobs. The school system should stop being disingenuous and appreciate the fact that as long as it continues to grade success by the result slip and fail to acknowledge the true reality that it is making academic zombies, pupils who can't create anything unique or innovative to drive the economy but rather a piece of the unfinished puzzle to make a picture of a standstill economy. They need to initiate in the curriculum a program where every student is required to innovate a product that can serve the people. The program can have different levels of intensity depending on the level of education you are. I cannot urge a congruity to the above statement but rather educators and high officials to take a look into the program implementations. They do say the good die young, for the first time let's make an education system that creates industries and employment that propels the economy towards sustainability. It is no secret to the success of the Western Economies they managed to benefit greatly from innovation from the education sector. Bill Gates at Harvard University created Microsoft that makes billions of dollars per year, Mark Zuckerberg at Harvard University created Facebook that makes billion yearly, Thomas Edison made the light bulb, Einstein started a branch of physics and contributed greatly to modern physics. These were students at various educational institutions that provided enough support and programs that enabled companies and inventions to be made. The same can be duplicated for our educational system. The Government can't create industries but industries and chemical processes are a result of the application of information learned and mastered at school. Without mastery, it means we are making our pupils cram and pass an exam and that's the reason why they can't use their knowledge to uplift their economy. Rather they move out to already existing economies to have lower-end jobs so that they get a decent salary. Zimbabwe as l have observed it has no value addition in education and it doesn't take a genius to point out the fact that, it's the reason why our mining industry and farming industry are one of the most affected. We need to send excess doctors, engineers, lawyers, and economists to mention but a few and not students. I don't wish to blandish your already existing beliefs but just point out the truth. More than half of the students that we sent to get tertiary education don't return home to contribute to the GDP of the country but only to leave our economy dormant. Economic prosperity starts from its roots which are the education system then to the students as the branches. The fruits being the innovations that give thrust to the economy. I believe that the Zimbabwean Dream can be achieved and for the first time, university graduates will not alienate their motherland but rather find opportunities in solving our countries problems. School institutions should also appreciate the fact that the world is changing and technology as we know it is changing hence many avenues are now open for teacher-student interactions. There is a need to upgrade our classrooms and school to initiate more research platforms. This will not only prepare our students for future jobs but also give them a chance to appreciate how other economies are growing so that we as Zimbabwe can become fast followers to the rapidly changing world. Some platforms as offered by Google include an online classroom where student-teacher interaction is possible even at home. The great minds of the 20th century will have to create virtual classrooms to connect students from different schools worldwide so that information can be shared to better improve both the teacher and student understanding.

I believe if our schools progress in this manner we are destined to have a strong foundation that will prove to be the cradle of economic progression. It's not a fallacy for my assumptions that l have proven to be facts for the country of Zimbabwe.

CHAPTER2: THE FUTURE BEGINS

To be visionary as a leader means you can recognize where we are as a country and where we are going to be in the future due to observed trends in primary researched data and second researched data. For Zimbabwe looking at population growth forecast it shows that they are going to be approximately 17,596,446people in 2030 with 1.78% yearly change and -19.9migrant net and for 2050 approximately 23,947,923people with 1.29% yearly change. With the data that l have shown and the current coronavirus 2019 pandemic, it means the approximate projections for yearly change will be altered to favor a rapid increase in overall population in 2030 due to lack of contraceptives and birth control mechanisms by parents at home and access to health facilities due to lockdown as the government takes its attention on the pandemic. This gives us a rapid deduction of 25 million people in Zimbabwe by the year 2050. The increased population will have a general linear relation to rural-urban migration as well as urbanization in its respect. More than half of these people will be leaving in urban areas and their income levels will be approximately 5000, 00 USD, this is for the general population. This is not a flippant situation to the inane individuals ready for vitriol comments but the reality. With a large population in urban areas that can afford the basic commodities and those not so basic, it means we are in trouble if we fail to prepare. We are talking about a population that can afford to buy those home stands, those commodities such as television sets and motor vehicles to mention but a few. I will tell you what companies in the production sector would do, because it happens to be that, l am starting one. So our goal as Kesa Global Fuels is to produce our diesel and if the market is stressing my production sector as the CEO, l would encourage that the consumer is overprized to stabilize demand. This will work even though l personally know that l am going to suffer a decrease in sales and eventually get broke. If you know a company to venture into a business to get broke then please tell me so that l can draw the red line to all my utterances. Still referring to my co-pending subject matter since no company wants to get broke they will keep producing these commodities at the unstable market price. If they don't adjust their industrial capabilities they won't meet demand. Forgive me but l will always condone businesses that bilk the consumer. This is because they lack the goal to supply the product and rather become the best in championing their profits whilst reverting to methods that place the consumer at a standstill point. This method is trite because it always accelerates the life cycle of a company to its death. This will reduce the GDP of the country if the company was one of the powerhouse sectors. Reverting to my summoned points, I came up with a long list of the needs of the 20th century for my country Zimbabwe. After our forefathers gave up their lives to fight for our independence, it is no doubt that they did not only fight for the land alone but also for air rights. For if they had fought for the land alone as they proclaimed to be doing, I believe they never thought about how climate change was going to revolutionize farming as we know it in its nature. Back to my subject matter, the list is as follows:

1. Demand for energy
2. Need for jobs
3. Need for school facilities
4. Demand for commodities
5. Demand for land for farming
6. Need for transport systems
7. Need for food
8. Need for freshwater
9. Need for fuel
10. Need for housing
12. Need for a digital cemetery
14. Need for space exploration and planetary acquisitions
16. Need for climate response teams?

Threats to come to include:
1. Bank security
2. Health security

The above information shown is just the tip of the iceberg and more information can be added by other visionaries in the 20th century. The list shows the primary needs that need drastic attention if we are to sail through the wave of the coming storm. If we are to make our coming challenge a zephyr we need to implement these systems that I am going to describe and start the journey of wealth creation rather than poverty reduction.

CHAPTER3: DEMAND FOR ENERGY

With an increase in the number of people in urban areas, they are going to require an energy system to supply the prolific population. We cannot continue to believe that Hwange Thermal Power Station and Kariba Hydropower station are going to be enough to power cities. This has been evident due to our current import of electricity from Eskom in South Africa. It doesn't take a genius to point out that our energy sector is struggling to supply 14 million people with electricity because the assistant of its local power was supplied from sub-power stations in the country. Now before our discussed figure of 25 million people in 2050, our energy sector will be stretched too thin, and exceeding blackouts in cities will become new normality. Companies in the informative sector that conduct online business will lose large dollars in profit and also owe many private and public stakeholders millions in debt. Since l am not going to dwell more on the problems but divide my objective effectively to also bring solutions to the spotlight. The issue of power sustainability has been launched in the country with a slightly better approach. This is not a blatant lie as solar energy has also been taking form in the energy sector with its potential promising economic growth. I have to point out certain outflows; these include energy systems that are not ventured. Wind energy has not yet been tested but to better create an adequate supply of energy we need innovators to investigate and prove theories that will enable new forms of power as we progress to acquire nuclear energy. On the subject matter of innovators, the country needs to start Energy Research Institutes to better tackle the problem of energy and also make international partners in the key field. To share ideas and better assess the power crisis before it becomes too big to handle practically. Remember l didn't say financially it can't be handled but will only cause an increase in liability due to electricity imports.

The other important aspects we have to focus on include power distribution. It's not enough to just create an energy system but l believe in the abnegation of an energy system with at its backbone a diverse power distribution mechanism. Since the population has increased. Space to use our pylons won't be enough as some of the building structures will be elevated. Wireless electricity is the key concept to adapt from the advent of the near field of cell phones to the advanced far-field technology. This will not only see our energy sector saving costs in transmission cables but advancing in a more clean and safe transmission process. The travesty to the above-mentioned technology is that it requires more research to prove the algorithms and Government or private sector funding for it to blossom.

CHAPTER4: DEMAND FOR LAND FOR FARMING

 Due to an increase in population, it means for the first time they are going to be land scarcity in a country when the whole liberation war was on land. Not to worry, the people of Zimbabwe have another greatest asset in their pocket. This asset is our minds and to be able to use it as a tool to generate solutions should be our main interest in the 20th Century. So before my investigation that l conducted in 2019. I deduced that to utilize the land we need to revolutionize the way we farm by creating elevated designs of our farms as l will illustrate below.

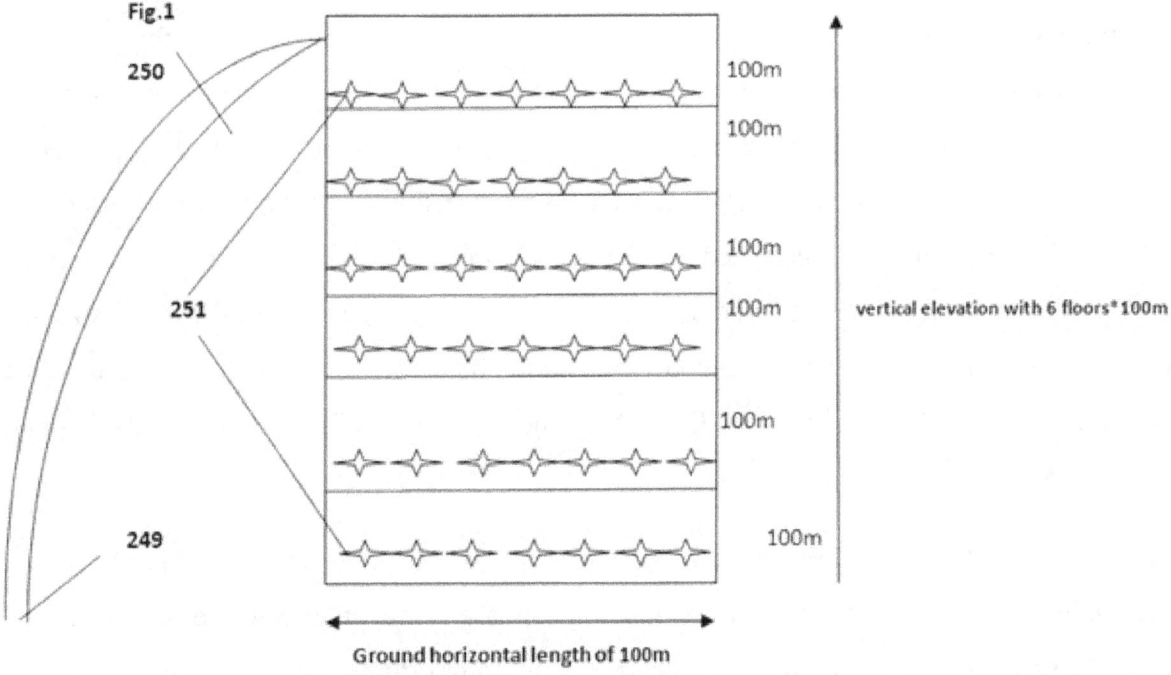

Fig.1 Reference for better understanding these farms as illustrated, 1 ha of ground farming will give us 6 ha to plant our crops. The elevated view can be applied to the whole farm and 251 are the plants, 249 is the water piping. Due to prolific information globally and to the competitions that I participated in they offered an eclectic mix of courses that encouraged me to come up with the design. Alteration of length and width of the floor levels dependent on the size of the farm

and how you would like to modularize it to produce desired segments. I am not trying to denigrate the ordinary day farmer but only provide a better solution if they wish for Zimbabwe to earn its title of being the breadbasket of Africa.

From those with pending questions on how the plants will access sunlight. I say the surface floor levels will be having transparent surface floor bases to allow photosynthesis to occur. Since it's a competition for global wealth rather than poverty reduction we need to be at the top of our game. The sunlight will always present a travesty at night. Due to my intelligent researches, I found out that alteration of the plant structure can only be achieved by changing the light frequency. This means that we can finally grow crops that Zimbabwe never dreamt of possible on its soils. The water ph is also monitored. No more exporting food from abroad and we can even grow our investigative crops and enable that our people are well fed.

By adopting this form of planting strategy we are not only investing in agriculture and sustainable land use but we are investing more in our people. This is done to feed those multitudes in our cities 10-20 years from now. In our process of becoming a wealth powerhouse, we need to connect our farmers to a dynamic market system. All farm products must not be allowed to be sold in their raw forms but rather value addition must be connected to the product. The creation of strong markets of different products is needed in Zimbabwe. Farmers need to be linked with their market. We also need a digital system that farmers can access to see the current market price of their product and where it is needed. Since the population of the people would have increased, it means they will be global completion of supplying to the market from both the local community and foreign farmers. Our farmers need to prepare for the worst whilst hoping for the best.

We need to create a convivial market for our farmers if we are to become an economic powerhouse. The threat behind a large population increase is that other countries are also expanding and they are going to channel their strength into intruding the highest paying markets in other countries. Hence if Food Security is our biggest strength they will look for our shortcomings to gain our market. Demand for land for farming is going to be the future talk. Our ability to recognize that what we hold precious today might not be there tomorrow creates a new possibility, reasoning, and creative thinking to say what are we going to do to earn food? What are the people going to eat? Are we going to produce enough?

Fig.2

The above figure shows a budded mango tree plant sample and a tomato. These were my samples to test the effect of light frequencies on crop growth rate.

Fig .3

The figure above showed a positive plant growth in this artificial growth housing. The crop was exposed for 2 weeks without sunlight but infrared light.

Fig .4

The above figure shows the complete growth room set up.

Fig.5

It's showing how the system is supporting micro plant life to add to the bio diversity.

CHAPTER5: NEED FOR FOOD

The above mention method is capable to provide us with the carbohydrates and vitamins that we will need in the future and to be able to acquire our proteins we need to have a different view than the first one. We have to ask ourselves what the Asians did. As we have observed generally land to rear these cattle and other general farm animals won't be available. Asians ended up eating seafood and some reverting to bugs and dogs to mention but a few. This is a clear indicator that a source of protein in the future is going to be a talk. Zimbabwe needs to prepare if it's going to feed a multitude of its growing population.

Some countries are investing more money in cellular meat production. I am talking about a situation where they are no more cattle but rather the cattle cells are multiplied to continue providing meat. This type of meat is best because no more ground feeding the cattle. The government can better yet advance its Biology sector by introducing the Animal cellular replication Research Institute. It can partner with university graduates so that it can better exploit its academic assets. This method won't only be an action intended to aggrandize the country in food production but at the core of our ambition to feed our people.

We have to think of the disadvantage of a population with high purchasing power. This means that unbalanced diets will be the talk of the decade. Zimbabwe needs to be ready for diabetic diseases, coronary heart diseases. Above all, we need to assess the disease distribution concerning age. The Health Sector and the Food production and distribution department need to work hand in hand and must be cognizant of the boundaries within which they work. We can no longer afford to approach our problems cheaply. It will generally be vividly recognized that our dependent elderly citizens will be the ones most affected. I am not an iconoclast but my points are only a true representation of the future.

Food can't be approached in the way we see it today for the elderly population in Zimbabwe but rather they should eat a personalized diet. How this will be handled 10-20 years from now it's up to the 20th century great minds. Distribution needs to be regularized and solving this problem will create an income source for our country due to imports of these finished products. What we have been doing since independence, will always make us poor as a nation because that is commodity selling. That is what our forefathers did and if we continue in that pathway we are not growing. To move up the economic ladder we need to sell products but above most solve our problems. Gone are the days when Zimbabweans have charity jobs, charity industries but rather let's advocate for wealth creation rather than poverty reduction.

CHAPTER6: NEED FOR FUEL

My cupidity in transportation has led me to invest my time and money in mentors and resources to conclude my theoretical fuel-producing mechanisms on paper and using the scientific method and intelligent researches to prove my hypothesis practically. My zeal and passion led me to be amongst the top inventors of the 20th century, now back to my laconic subject matter of fuel in 10-20 years to come. I have a non-congruity notion on the point that Henry Ford's invention should be put in the garage for good but l see an opportunity for Zimbabwe to find a better alternative for crude fuel that is renewable to use. This will influence a political movement since some countries earn 90% of their GDP via crude oil exports but a frog lip can enable our country to be a beneficiary of their fuel. Now economically this will enable a rapid steep growth since crude oil imports cause a large unbalance in trade annually.

I will try to avoid exhorting my ideas by allowing critical thinking rather than passive thinking to the reader. Another way to fight fuel is to implement electric motor vehicles in our industries or other vehicles that are independent of fuel. Since our population would have increased, it means an increase in purchase power amongst the citizens. An average individual can now afford a car our imports of crude oil will be forced to expand hence if action is not taken an economic recession will take form.

The government and other private and public stakeholders need to invest their money in finding solutions to fuel issues in the country. If this method means that other industries are emerging in Zimbabwe to serve as a remedy to our problems, then let it be. Government officials should not spend billions of dollars on sourcing fuel in other countries. This will only make us poor as a nation. That's the mindset that will make us a charity country. Rather they should focus on empowering research and innovations that enable us to be industrially dependent and market diversified. Before my subject matter as observed in earlier discussions, if we fail to prepare our fuel industry, we might be heading to become the poorest nation in the African continent but don't fear the book is called The Zimbabwean Dream, and reading and implementation is the tool for wealth creation.

Fig.6

The above image is showing the alternative for diesel that l produced at an institution in Mutare called Saint Augustine's High (Tsambe)

Fig.7

The fuel products made after some time to settle are shown above.

CHAPTER7: ECONOMIC GROWTH IN ZIMBABWE

Zimbabwe since independence has invested its resources in the following sectors which include education, farming, mining, and tourism. It has allowed specialization rather than diversification in its economical structure. You rarely find economic uplift in a country such as this. We are known under SADAC for food security and we have been good at producing enough food to feed our population before the risk multiplier such as droughts and floods attacked our dear continent. I remember when l had the chance to lead the whole school; it wasn't the same as leading myself because alone l could practically achieve anything and in the least possible amount of time. The challenge became to drive every person on the same vision of academic excellence. This meant that everyone had to be disciplined, punctual, and have the same enthusiasm to drive through challenges. Above all, we had to complement each other in terms of skills if we had to sail through and practically achieve our goal.

Zimbabwe is no different from my above-mentioned situation because, for economic growth, different sectors in the economy need to complement each other.10-20 years from now we need to make sure that our ordinary farmer is no longer using ox-drawn plough for ground tilling because how can you connect the farming sector to other sectors in the economy such as financing, logistics, and insurance. As observed this has created a large gap in-between different sectors of the economy. Since l pointed out that complementing each other is the true secret to economic growth, l need to tell you the effect of lack of complementing each other to the economic growth. Before my subject matter, lack of complementing each other will lead to a huge difference between the top class, middle class, and lower class of the society. Since the ordinary farmer is now benefiting alone, the top class will be dominated by people in the farming sector and the middle class will have less to almost no one in the financial sector and insurance sector. This will affect our economy because lack of a strong middle class will lead to a small number of people contributing to the national GDP hence if their business model crumbles our virtual economy will generate bugs and crash.

Now an economic system that is complementary to each other is pictured to a farmer using a tractor and a combined harvester. The farmer has an insurance package for his tractor and also for his harvester. Now the farming sector is connected to the Financial sector. The products are now benefiting both the two sectors. This will enable both the strengthening of the top class and middle class to hence produce rapid economic growth.

It's not enough to add value to a commodity and hope that our economy will prosper but we need to assess our product distribution, product linkage, and basic frame of reference from other products. We can't continue to focus on food security as our only prospering sector but rather diversify our products. We need to make a connection between sectors to allow our middle class to expand. Product distribution involves identifying products in each province and how we can create sectors that make the whole country connected. This l personally observed during my leadership at school.

Another point is adaptability and this means that making products is great and all but what's better is advancing our industries to produce the product in the shortest period, using less energy, fewer materials as possible, faster processing devices. This opens new sectors in the economy to link with our advanced industries and hence expand our network of economic growth. Growth is not rapid but it takes time if carefully studied and researches are taken but at their backbone are shaped by the 20th century great minds that are ready for implementations.

10-20 years from now we need not only to create a few products but many products and this means a diverse hemisphere of consumers and the public goods. I won't sugarcoat the situation by saying it's enough but it will surely prove effective. Now Zimbabwe has many products being created. We need to also introduce more products that didn't exist before also being complemented by new technology. We have been focusing on products that any simple nation can make but for our future economic growth, it means Zimbabwe is not only food security and the breadbasket of the world but the battery of Africa, African fuel, and African telecommunication hub to mention but a few.

I questioned myself, why we had all the global technology in our figure tips but yet we were not implementing and using them. It then hit me that technology was not the problem but rather our mindsets. By mindset, l mean our creative portion of our brains. We have ¾ portion of the whole production sector population that can't forge anything in their minds but rather complain about how we are poor as a nation. These inane statements need to back up by industrial production for me to finally draw the line to my statements.

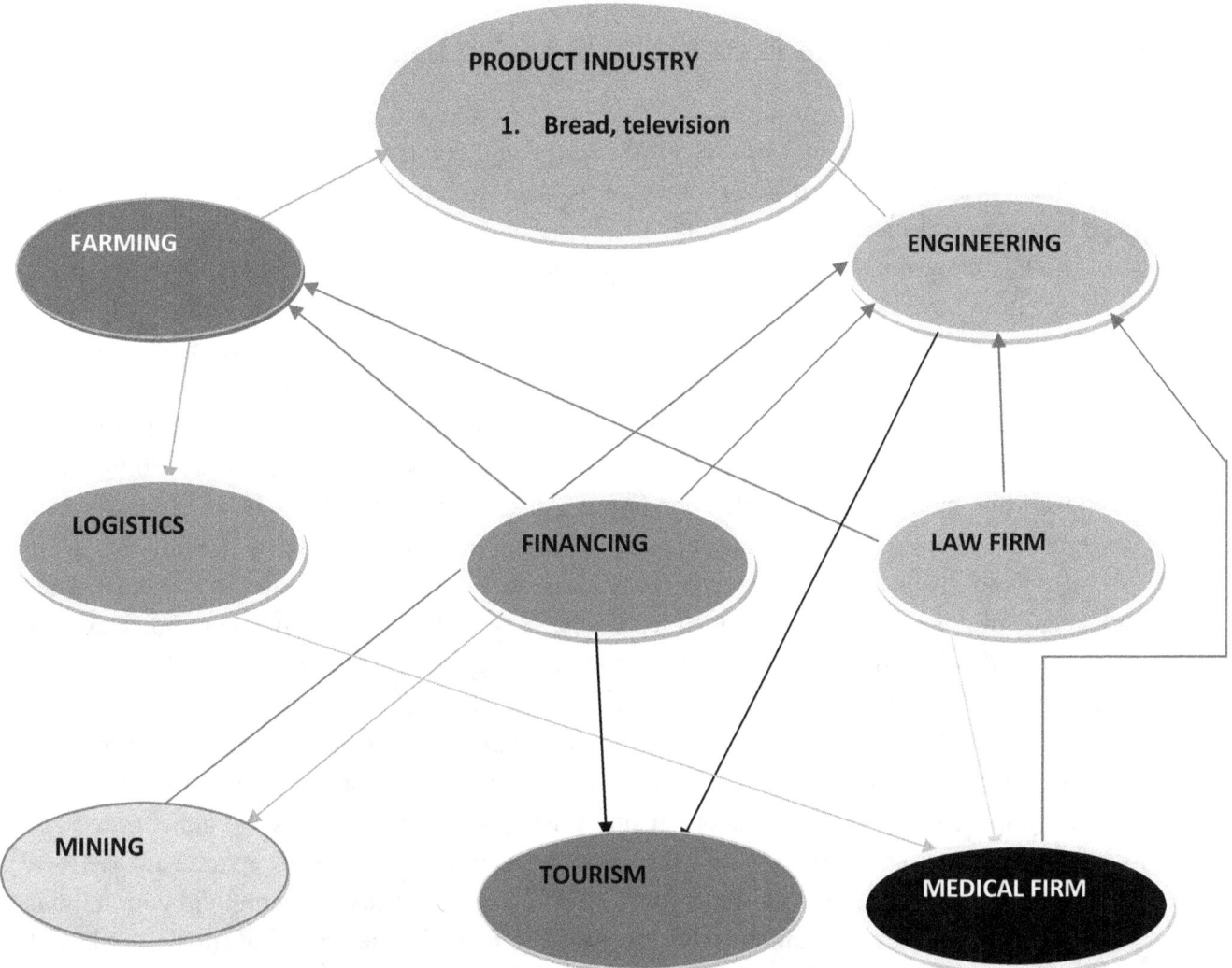

Fig.8

The Zimbabwean product space needs to complement each other if there is going to be economic growth. The diagram shows our sectors and the arrows show linkage in sectors. Without this network, we will end up with a stretched economic class and a few people occupying the top class and the rest at the lower class.

–

CHAPTER 8: NEED FOR A DIGITAL CEMETERY

I can't be arrogant at this need because of the human culture that precedes all of us. The need to bury our loved ones has been a long-time practice and to come and say that the practice has to stop is a non-congruity amongst individuals. As we have just observed from the coronavirus pandemic it showed that if death rates increase it stresses both resources and mostly land. In 10-20 years from now 25 million people will need burial sites and adequate calculations will show you that our burial sites are not going to be enough and we need to advocate technology to our problem.

No more can we say physical graveyard but we have to initiate a virtual graveyard. The point of novelty behind this digital system is that it will save space, historical records accessibility, and less distortion due to natural weather conditions. This is achieved by the following descriptive information. People enter data and the system captures and stores the information. In this digital space, people can add stories of their deceased relative by uploading a video and pictures. The advantage of this system is that a video representative of a person will have more impact on the living. Another benefit is that a new generation of the digital cemetery can have other employment opportunities in digital data analyst and history specification.

The land is a valuable asset and in 10-20 years, we might not have enough for all our needs. We need to generate solutions for how we are going to deal with its scarcity. The best solution for cemetery space is to adopt a digital burial site. With the memory of drives and general storage disks increased to terabytes, the whole of Zimbabwe's digital data can be captured at ease. Before my above-mentioned subject matter, the bigger question that is roaming in your mind is what about the bodies. Cremation is the next best alternative to the grappling situation. Since it takes time, the cremation sites need to be increased in the country, or better yet the cremation process bettered for a faster process.

10-20 years from now our most valuable commodity is going to be our brains and using our brains as a tool will soon be evident to idle minds of the society that it's our greatest asset. The digital cemetery is open for improvements by the 20th century great minds.

CHAPTER 9: NEED FOR A TRANSPORT SYSTEM

Now we have multitudes of people traveling daily from city to city and the bigger question is how will we do that and better yet how effectively can we achieve that. Our population will need transport for daily commuting and if we concentrate our money on the personal car and fuel, it will only lead to road congestions and reduced productivity hence economic retardation. What we need to do is find a fast transport system, occupy large people and is crude oil-free. For Zimbabwe 10-20 years from now, this transport can be a bus that uses electrical power or better yet electrical trains.

Generally, our railway is not up to standard, this means that new rail tracks and trains need to be implemented. A challenge posed to the 20th century great minds will prove to be a frog leap to the transport sector in 10-20 years to come. We must be cognizant of the need to give a transport system to our prolific population for a more productive population without the travesty of transport in their operations. Improvements need to be added regularly to the new initiative for it to last long.

Before my summoned points in chapter 3 on demand for energy, the energy sector will complement the transport sector in the provision of electricity. This is because for the mass transport system to have life it must be using energy. Since our transport sector will be a subsidiary of the energy sector or rather a beneficiary they need to maintain a close relationship amongst the two industries.

The transport sector needs to offer an eclectic mix of transport modes. This means a specialization in the railway system alone is not the solution but diversifying our means will give a variety and referring to chapter 7, economic growth. The idea of a personalized transport system will mainly be luxury. To fit all the aspects of renewability and using the nationally available resources in a mass transport system is the way to go. To all the people that want or would alter for faster horses than a car, 1 am not an Iconoclast. I am only trying to shed a little light on the economic situation and offer a lasting remedy to our foreseen predicament.

The private and public sector needs to look into these challenges to generate a solution for the future. Careful analyses of monetary inflows and outflows need to be considered as a planning stage as this will avoid embezzlement.

CHAPTER 10: CULTURE, UNITY AND GOVERNANCE

They do say when countries develop they westernize so generally the west did not need to learn the African culture because after colonization we left it all behind. My people did all this in anticipation to gain what the white man had forged in our environment and forgot that sticking to their own culture in this quest would have made their victory more certain. In their quest, they lost one thing that our forefathers had created and maintained for centuries. This key concept is unity.

Without unity, they are no complementary effort hence a country's production is lowered. We have individuals with all the resources but they cannot share with others because they think a candle can lose its light by lighting other candles. These beliefs are a result of a lack of unity amongst our people and they need to be promulgated for change to take form. The reason that l have addressed these issues in one discussion is that they are all beneficiaries of one another. So we need a culture for there to be unity and unity for there to be good governance. We can't fix the scars of governance by bandages in the future because that will never heal it.

What did culture do to our people before colonization? It excluded the issue of identifying each other by race. Without this subsidiary identification, we lived in harmony as one people. Hence family ties were not bound to the family alone but also to the community. People would come to work at the chief's field not in a pejorative manner because they were not getting a sum of payment but because they worked so that food is available for the community and not for oneself alone. Great Zimbabwe was not built in one day and it wasn't built by one person. If it were so then that national monument wouldn't be grounded in Zimbabwe. Some are obdurate and still keep all their resources to themselves but even the smartest and most capable individual without any technological help wouldn't build the Great Walls of Zimbabwe by himself or herself.

Unity amongst our people will ignite good governance. What this means is above all straightforward. If the people are united they will have different opinions but their judgments and choice won't be farfetched from each other. These choices are influenced by the community in which they reside and the community by the culture and since the culture is the same the output reaction is always the same or slightly incremented but without any overall effect.

Before my point of governance now we move into the future .10-20 years from now as our population would have exploded our governing structure doesn't need to operate in a central point for example Harare. We need to implement a stretched governance and this implies a strong leadership in each megacity or eventually, the government will lose control of the people and the result is a focus on petty political issues rather than economical resuscitation. This is a more diverse topic for another time.

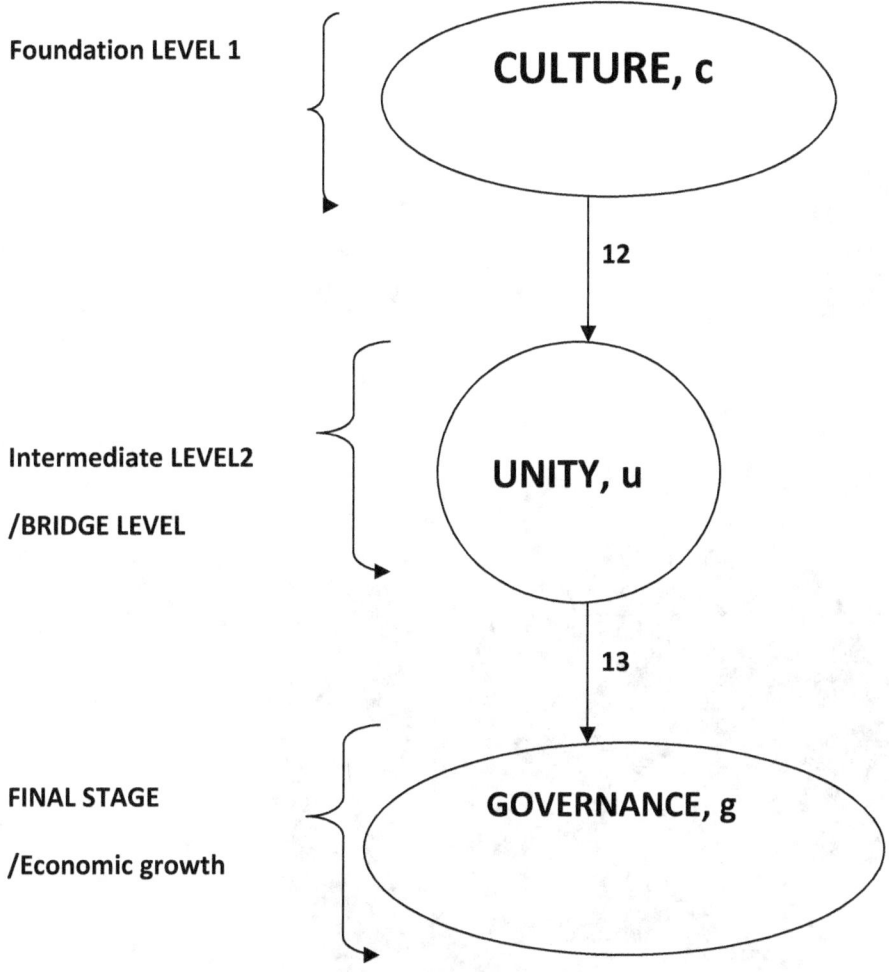

Foundation LEVEL 1

CULTURE, c

12

Intermediate LEVEL2

/BRIDGE LEVEL

UNITY, u

13

FINAL STAGE

/Economic growth

GOVERNANCE, g

Fig.9

Before my above diagram, to enable true trinity in movement, economic progression can't exist without an intermediate, unity. Without unity level 1 and level 3 can't connect.**13**Process flow can continue even without culture. The diagram shows the basic limits of operation of each element in economic growth.

12Basically show how culture is linked with unity. Every separate entity is needed to fit the puzzle of economic growth. In the future when things are not in alignment we have to find which element is out of alignment so that we can get it in place then everything will be fine. But for future reference, we need to recognize that no entity exists in isolation hence **peoples culture** has people who keep it, national monuments, traditional leaders, museums, and **unity** its people binding that culture to be part of their core principle whereas **governance** is the laws, legislation that guides these people and protection of this culture. As l think most of you have seen that people are basic constituents of all entities hence people's choices are above all considered in each entity shift.

Intersection of the three entities is **people**

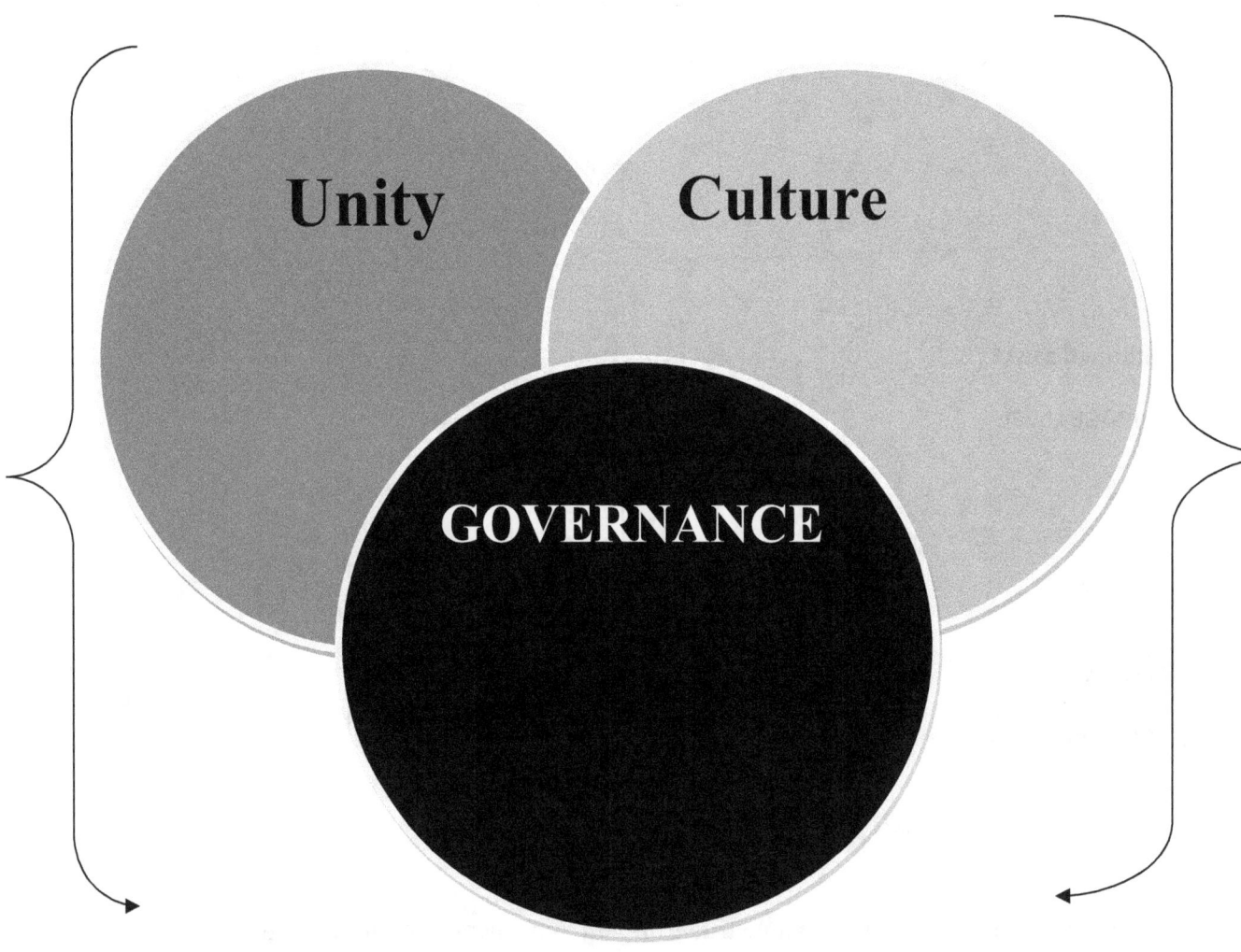

CHAPTER 11: NEED FOR HOUSING

From the dawn of time, human beings have been an ambitious race. The Zimbabwean people on the other hand have been defined by endless quests to find a proper home. Our great desire made us shift from leaving in caves and being nomadic to build the great walls of Zimbabwe and other 'madzimbahwe' or houses. Our people for a long time accepted their newly found home and up to this time we have lived in this housing structure and faced no problems. The ability to think about the future and how the population growth is going to expand in the coming years vividly points out the fact that our housing structure needs revising if it is to have life in the future. I believe that people are too comfortable in their current cradle but to move forward as a nation and as a continent we need to change and progress.

I believe one tangible resource that we didn't utilize as a nation is air rights. I don't wish to exhort the upcoming statement but we can't keep using the residential housing planning strategy that was developed in the 1990s because it wasn't meant for a large population as the one that is going to be part of our community. The first stage before venturing into this housing planning strategy is to create a new foundation for our community. We need a foundation that allows utilization of both the ground and the air rights for housing sustainability. Let me try to elucidate my summoned point on air rights as some might think that l am advocating a housing plan that is ubiquitous as the skyscraper buildings. Skyscraper buildings we already have but are they going to serve our needs in the coming years? The answer to that question is both yes and no. The answer is yes in the sense of mass human housing capabilities and no in the sense of flexibility. Let's take a practical situation of everyone living in skyscraper buildings. How will everyone maneuver in and out of the building? How will electricity be distributed in these skyscraper buildings? How will parcel delivery be conducted? The beauty of a personal car in this generation era is that road congestions are few and home parking is the daily norm. All the questions that l have asked have made others think about architectural designs that will make all the problems that l have pointed disappear. To customize our skyscraper buildings to serve our community needs will be the perfect housing strategy for our society. Other broad questions that erupted in your brains will soon be answered in the following chapters.

CHAPTER 12: NEED FOR FRESH WATER

Zimbabwe currently has water shortages and it's a result of fewer water sources and it has been a result of growth in population and allocation of housing stands to places without any viable water source or too many people in a place of fewer water sources. Both scenarios were a leading factor in the crisis that we face today. From a scientific perspective, 70% of the water is trapped in ice form and is trapped in the Polar Regions. We only have 25% readily to our use. Our primary focus isn't only to utilize the 25% water for our community by drilling 1000 boreholes in the country or building dams alone. If Henry Ford had asked people what they wanted they would have said they wanted faster horses rather than the car. If this was the right way to go then why hasn't it made us the richest continent in the world? It's because every country in the world is doing that and because it's an overcrowded market already and it exists at the bottom of the food chain. Countries in the west have shifted from rainwater to seawater. They have done this because it's hard, it's there, and because it is unutilized. We need to find other means to make water and utilize them if we are to survive in the future. We have become too comfortable in the present situation that our dependence on a specialized source of water has made us lazy to think of other methods to make a sustainable water source for ourselves. From chapter one l have stated it as **MY DREAM**. This is because Zimbabweans are the only people with whom l have learned that they forget their dreams soon after primary level of schooling. Like school uniforms, they became the same in producing answers in an examination and also in job careers. They act as if their life destiny books are the same. They are few individuals that emerge from any group. I have to tell all Zimbabweans that they shouldn't be afraid of life and taking a little risk because that's the only way that they will progress as a nation. When you take big positive risks for the betterment of others only two things happen and number one it's that you win and the other one is that you learn. Believe me, you never fail because the one who chooses to fail is the one who has the guts to quit. They are a quote that says that It's only impossible until it is done. It's only impossible for Africa or better yet Zimbabwe to have water sustainability until someone does make it a reality. In the future, we don't need to be the nation that imports water from our neighboring countries because we failed to prepare and make our dream a reality today. For our economy to have life intelligent researches need to be done and partnerships made rather than for it to be on life support.

CHAPTER 13: NEED FOR SCHOOL FASCILITIES

Thanks to the President of the Republic of Zimbabwe, Honorable Emmerson Dambudzo Mnangagwa he introduced education 5.0 in our school institutions that are encouraging innovation as clearly seen during the coronavirus pandemic. This education system enabled our country to save lives and emerge an industry in our educational facilities. Truly l can't be an ingrate and fail to appreciate how this initiate has overlapped boundaries of education and practical application. This was a repulsive gap that no force had been able to close. Now before my chapter heading, the education sector had not been able to get every student in a classroom and this is evident from the increase in the informal sector. People currently trading without a working permit and not paying tax to the government. The cycle is very simple really in the sense that if the tertiary education fees aren't cost-effective the informal trading parent can't enable to take his or her child to university and the last resort is joining the family business. It's a known fact that the informal sector will never die out unless every child is in a classroom. It doesn't matter whether it's a child from a rural area or an urban area but every child in a classroom. Now 10-20 years from now as the population would have increased it will be difficult to get every student in a classroom and even to those privileged they won't even get access because our school facilities won't be enough. The world was blessed by the covid 19 pandemics because it gave us the chance to practically built and put these systems to the test. We need to place these systems permanently so that every child gets in the classroom in the future. More investments need to be placed in the interesting field of virtual reality and synchronized technology including real-time conferences and classrooms. Learning from home will become the new norm in the future and an increase in-home tutoring will be evident in the coming years. Our subsidiary sector in the operation will be our daily classroom that needs remodeling and restructuring so that they can occupy more students and at the same time enable a learning environment that is student-friendly. From my earlier chapter on housing strategies, they can also be applied to schools hence complementation of both sectors. Our priority is building a wealthy nation is placing our people at heart first and not generating quick fixes to our problems but rather destroying the roots of the problem. Our school facilities will need this change if we are to be ready for the future.

CHAPTER 14: DEMAND FOR COMMODITIES

With the prolific population, an increase in rural-urban migration, and a population with high purchasing power the demand for commodities is going to be high. Industries in the production sector need to increase output to meet the expanded population or rather face a decline in customer interactions as people will be flooded in foreign markets. The result of this will lead to excessive loss of foreign currency in the country thereby rendering our local currency powerless. We can't only focus on food production but also on food substitutes. Protein and milk substitutes are needed and the technology to do so is available with the credit of international scientists but improvements and alterations are still open to any innovator with the dream to make our future brighter. Due to better jobs, people will be having a higher income flow hence the demand for energy, housing, luxury goods will become a daily norm that's why l covered those in the earlier chapters since they were our main demands. Commodity trade destroyed our economy as earlier as our vegetable market emerged and the product market never grew. They will be commodity demand as l elucidated but that commodity in terms of the food industry needs to be rooted at its backbone with the product market. These two markets need to work as one body and from the chapter on economic growth be complementary to other sectors so that they is diversification rather than specialization. By commodity substitution, we will be adding a new product from our ordinarily existing commodity leading to a complicated product that we can exploit and export to other countries. That complicated product will enable Zimbabwe to make other complicated products making other countries fast followers to our initiatives. Taking this into a more practical contest if Zimbabwe was to make its cars it will mean that advancement in making buses and trucks will be easy. But to those countries taking the first initiative in making a truck might have troubles because of the lack of the expanded knowledge. Right now we face problems in our product market and this is evident from the Zimbabwean citizens in many crossing the border to buy sugar and salt to mention but a few. These products are the ones that exist at the bottom of the food chain and must be readily available in our country. The problem is not product beneficiation because we have been able to do that but increasing our product space so that we have a variety of products in our economy. Lack of this expanded product space is an indication that our education is not focusing on uplifting various sectors but rather the most paying at the moment. This will only make our school students gold diggers rather than problem solvers.

CHAPTER 15: NEED FOR CLIMATE RESPONSE TEAMS

Cyclone Idai that destroyed most of the Chimanimani area in Zimbabwe was an eye-opener on the need for a climate response team. Due to global warming, our planet has been affected drastically and pointing fingers at the causes is a thing of the past and we are now in an era of awareness and action. Too much damage has already been made and for us to sit on our hands and think that planting trees alone will prevent us from the upcoming weather hazards it's a reverie. Regionally these climatic response teams will not only assist in the occurrence of a natural disaster but will also be ready to take in climatic refugees from other countries in their respective countries. This initiative needs to be done immediately for us to be prepared for an unexpected occurrence like the one we encountered of the non-quotidian cyclone. People have a perception of taking action in trying to solve the problem whilst it is in progress and when it has reached critical stages but preparation is the best solution in diverting from that path. With the advent of technology, we are blessed as a nation because information availability is limitless and people can now know where these disasters have occurred in the least amount of time possible and the response team can assist before death and starvation pick up the first call. Community mobilizes need to be organized to teach people movement procedures and above all safety precautions. Social media can act as a fast means of promulgating information to the general public. We can't continue to be a nation that feeds on handouts but rather champions assisting other nations at large. Our problems have made us always look towards international organizations for support leading to our people not being creative to solve their problems. I don't wish to denigrate any cherished beliefs on international assistance but advocate for self-reliance and less assistance. The climate response teams can work with the local government to enable complementary effort.

The future is a blessing to those who prepare for it now because it will prevent unnecessary catastrophe to biodiversity. Climatic change is like a spinning wheel that can't be stopped but rather measures to reduce its effects need to be put in place. Food and housing for these climatic refugees need to be in place and our ability to create these sustainable housing and food sources as clearly been mentioned in the earlier chapters will be a great leap for our communities. Climatic change will be discussed as a threat in a future chapter and the remedies to climate change will clearly be stated. Now it's up to the next generation of foresight practitioners to champion progress in this field of climatic awareness and human protection by implementing this system into practice.

CHAPTER 16: NEED FOR JOBS

Due to an increase in the number of graduates in the country our citizens are going to need jobs to serve the community. Recently more than 30% of the youth are unemployed and the numbers are rising rapidly. The solution to this problem is job marketing and this can be achieved by the government if it allows its civil servants to work in other countries. The government has invested greatly in education but in this era, it's not benefiting from that investment. Our neighboring countries might be lacking doctors or teachers and dispatching these people in various countries will earn the country foreign currency and in the process reduce the current unemployment rates. The future is exciting for our people and by creating all these above-mentioned needs will emerge industries in the country that will employ our people. Our people have been faced with a mindset that has destroyed us for as long as I could remember. This mindset is based on the fact that the government will create the industries that the people will work in. I have mentioned in an earlier chapter that the people responsible for technological advancements and industrialization are the academics because they are the ones with the practical know-how. It's not mendacious for me to point out that new jobs are going to emerge in 10-20 years to come. Our government has invested greatly in industrialization and failed to know that the coming era is about technological advancement. The multifarious industries in the countries need to adopt smart systems and technology such as virtual reality and artificial intelligence to enable fast processing of information and goods production. Some isolated jobs will begin to take shape in the economy. Our ability to invest in these systems won't only make us grow economically but will make our youth and above all citizens have jobs. Our job industry will be influenced and colored by how many problems we will solve. It's our innovators that will solve our deepest and unanswered problem thereby create jobs for our citizens. The jobs that we create for ourselves are the only ones that will add greatly to our economy.

CHAPTER 17: NEED FOR SPACE EXPLORATION AND PLANETARY AQUISITIONS

I can feel my adrenaline rise as l read the above heading. Space Exploration and Planetary Acquisition are a primary necessity for the future of Zimbabwe to meet its goal. I know that currently our airlines are facing problems and they also need solving but that's not my concern today. Let's talk about the benefits and opportunities for space exploration. The human race has faced great discoveries and experiences and the belief that a man can go to the moon was unfounded. It took great men and women to make the first moon shot amazing. It became an inspiration to me also and with the global climatic change taking place to catch up with us may be the only chance for our race to avoid extinction is to become interplanetary. This is not science fiction but a reality. If our climatic response teams are not able to work complementary with the community, we might not be able to stop this climatic change. The issue of space exploration might not be a quotidian sector in Zimbabwe but it can grow in popularity if our citizens grow the curiosity to venture into that sector. So if we venture into space exploration we would have opened a new chapter of discovery to our people. Space exploration offers an opportunity for Zimbabweans to investigate other forms of life that might exist in the universe. They are different asteroids that might be a source of minerals and samples can be brought back on Earth for analysis and better yet for our utilization. For scientific purposes, some experiments that are not possible on earth are possible in space. They will be no limitations but an endless probability. Taking an in-depth view of organ printing, that is still going under test by NASA scientist based in the United States evidence is pointing that the experiment is successful in space conditions. The failure of the experiment on the Earth's conditions was caused by gravity and it resulted in the organ experiment being printed as a deformed lump rather than a perfect shape. In space they are no limitation caused by gravity and hence the shape of the organ isn't altered. Hence what l can say about space exploration is that Earth's limitations are all possibilities. Someone must be excited and thinking right now on how he or she can do this in Zimbabwe. We need to first admit to the fact that we can't start a watch factory at a place without watchmakers. Allow me to elucidate further on the summoned subject matter. Although starting this factory is possible, it is costly and would result in unnecessary loss of revenue. The first step is education and at its leaning pillar a system that supports that branch to prosper and financially rise. Space

Exploration isn't a branch that pays instantly but it requires an investment to make it work. A collaborative effort is needed and this isn't a fight for Zimbabwe alone but it's a continental fight. We need African Union to take a stand and be creative to start solving the big problems. We need to organize and strategize on our health care systems, education, energy, and food security but those problems are small and if we refuse to adapt and change, we won't grow as a continent. The bigger question to ask is how we can start to solve the big problems. It's never a matter of the task being financially feasible but a situation of courage and be ready to fail and using that setback as a frog leap to attaining our goal. We have a multitude of Zimbabwe making a daily routine of trying to succeed in whatever endeavor they have set their minds on but failing to accept to fail along the way. To them, I say they are not even trying. This space race will require a Zimbabwe that is ongoing, innovative, adaptive, fearless, and intellectually equipped to solve challenges that are to come. We can do this and as Mr. Knowledge Chikundi once said, "15 drops make a river". We only need to offer collaborative effort for our goal to become a reality. From the previous chapters, I have talked about unity and unity in a big project like this that overlaps from a country matter into a continental matter. This means as a continent we forget our differences and focus the core of our energy on creating a continent worth talking about and a global community worth praising. To those scientists who have already started in this venture or those finance houses that have already started pouring money to private entities that are into Space Exploration, keep the fire burning and never stop believing that those 15 drops will eventually make a river. To those that haven't started, all that I can say is that you now have the white paper and your effort will be the thrust to making Space Exploration and Planetary Acquisition alive for Zimbabweans and above all the global community at large.

THREATS:

<u>CHAPTER 18: BANK SECURITY</u>

The future of Zimbabwe will be shaped by our financial institutions and the ability to authenticate and carry out daily transactions at ease at a public or private effort. Our current financial system presents a challenge in authenticating funds internationally. This travesty is caused by the fact that the current trading institutions (banks) in Africa or specifically speaking, Zimbabwe don't have the confidence and true identity of account holders to enable the international bank to bank monetary exchange. This is evident because of the use of a centralized bank ledger in daily day-to-day transactions. The challenge that is posed by this banking strategy is that it is open to manipulation and with very little computing power an individual of my caliber and programming background can easily access the bank ledger and temper with transactions for my malicious intent. Another pressing issue is the inability to carry out 24hr/365days per year transacting system. All these above-identified problems for the best of reasons are all threats that lurk amid our financial sector. Using our ignorance in the face of an attack can prove to be a non-pertinent reason in the face of the real reality that we have lost our funds.

The solution that l am going to present is common to others but to some none existing. The financial banking institutions need to create a system of decentralized ledgers that allow simultaneous and synchronized authenticating of ongoing transactions. These ledgers will create the complexity in alteration of accounts and the confidence in account holders that their money is in safe hands. To make this dream a reality there is a need for a complementary effort from the public and the innovators of the 20th century. There is a need to create a network of users for the system to effectively work and this means getting every Zimbabwean engaged in the new banking strategy. This process of getting every Zimbabwean engaged can be accelerated by issuing tokens and interests to the referrals brought in by an individual. This will personally raise the awareness of the new banking strategy but in the same way, raise interest in the new system.

Forgive me for being too vociferous in presenting my point on the banking strategy but to clear the unpleasant atmosphere, let me just say that the banks don't need to do an abrupt implementation of this initiative without a strong network resource and this also includes huge amounts of computing power to mention but a few. The banking sectors also need to be equipped with the knowledge to control such complex systems at their end. In my conclusion on the topic, l can only say the success of the banking system involves adaptation and inclusiveness in transaction and account authentication.

CHAPTER 18: HEALTH SECURITY

The effort in making the Zimbabwean Dream is all channeled in our citizens. If the citizens are healthy then it means that they can be able to carry out their daily work with ease but the reverse means that they are great retardation in work effort and poor results at the end. The health security that l am trying to point out in this book involves making sure that disease research institutes are established in the country that propels graduates and researchers to find solutions to diseases that have for long been causing deaths in the country. Such diseases include diabetes and malaria to mention but a few. We can't continue to create academic professionals that are there to fill the job gaps but rather we should have these professionals advance the current medical situation that roams in the country. I can't stop illuminating that the country needs more problem solvers. We can't go anywhere if we are only good at solving small problems. I understand that trying to solve these big diseases that have caused the whole world to shift towards a negative trajectory can seem like searching for a needle in a haystack when the person searching for the needle doesn't even know the color of the needle. It is hard but because we are trying they isn't any greater joy for the author that we are part of something great and our effort will eventually be rewarded.

Health security is also in linkage with every citizen from early childhood to adulthood in each community to be given affordable and quality access to a health facility. Health facilities private or public need to be provided and the current situation elucidate that although health facilities are there in rural areas they are not providing quality service and l won't delve into the reason behind the occurrence but only point out that health security is needed if we are to have a strong and capable human capital as a nation. Health security for the nation can also be affected by the diet that the people are indulging in. This diet mainly involves genetic modification that in the long run can cause detrimental effects to the individual if not substituted by healthy foods. This means that an intelligent setup needs to be implemented by a public or private effort to combat these genetic modifications at the wholesale side to enable a transparent market base and health security.

In conclusion, the above needs and threats that are to be faced in the coming decades need to be addressed and we need to prepare as a nation Zimbabwe to harness all the opportunities that will come as a result of these needs and threats. To the other walks of life that seem that this book has been useful to act as a puzzle piece in their economies feel free to implement the solutions to your community.

Author biography

Hello, I am Kelvin Tanyaradzwa Saungweme a student, entrepreneur, social maverick as well as an academic achiever. My passion is an assemblage of both computer science and physics to forge my nonephemeral cupidity in the field of Space Exploration. I have many accomplishments locally and internationally in my name surreptitious due to hard work, obsession, and a keen desire to outdo my previous self. Before my co-pending laconic subject matter,l have approached patenting avenues for a device in my name with the field of the invention being alternative energy, to serve the local and global community at large to ease fuel shortage. With mentorship and resources, I hope to expand my knowledge to hence prolific inventions to help people above my benefit.

Achievements and Projects

1. 2019 South African Youth Engineering & Science Symposium Silver Medalist
2. 2019 Zimbabwe Science Fair Outstanding Achiever
3. 2020 Zimbabwe Science Fair Gold Medalist
4. 2020 Zimbabwe Science Fair Outstanding Achiever
5. 2020 YALE Science and Engineering Association Recipient
6. 2020 Think World Science Fair Zimbabwean Delegate

Projects

1) Sangweme balanced atmosphere 2.0 project
2) The Green Gold The Future project
3) Equation of Singularity Collapse theoretical work
4) The Zimbabwean Dream book
5) Visual Basics Programming Solutions book

www.ingramcontent.com/pod-product-compliance
Lightning Source LLC
Chambersburg PA
CBHW080628220526
45467CB00011B/3422